CW00494886

Ketogenic Vegetable

Recipes

Effective Low-Carb Recipes To Balance Hormones And Effortlessly Reach Your Weight Loss Goal.

Introduction

Do you want to make a change in your life? Do you want to become a healthier person who can enjoy a new and improved life? Then, you are definitely in the right place. You are about to discover a wonderful and very healthy diet that has changed millions of lives. We are talking about the Ketogenic diet, a lifestyle that will mesmerize you and that will make you a new person in no time.

So, let's sit back, relax and find out more about the Ketogenic diet.

A keto diet is a low carb one. This is the first and one of the most important things you should now. During such a diet, your body makes ketones in your liver and these are used as energy.

Your body will produce less insulin and glucose and a state of ketosis is induced. Ketosis is a natural process that appears when

our food intake is lower than usual. The body will soon adapt to this state and therefore you will be able to lose weight in no time but you will also become healthier and your physical and mental performances will improve.

Your blood sugar levels will improve and you won't be predisposed to diabetes. Also, epilepsy and heart diseases can be prevented if you are on a Ketogenic diet.

Your cholesterol will improve and you will feel amazing in no time.
How does that sound

A Ketogenic diet is simple and easy to follow as long as you follow some simple rules. You don't need to make huge changes but there are some things you should know.

So, here goes!

Now let's start our magical culinary journey!

Ketogenic lifestyle...here we come!

Enjoy!

Tasty Avocado Salad

This is very tasty and refreshing!

Preparation time: 10 minutes **Cooking time:** 0 minutes **Servings:** 4

Ingredients:
- 1 avocados, pitted and mashed
- Salt and black pepper to the taste
- ¼ teaspoon lemon stevia
- 1 tablespoon white vinegar
- 14 ounces coleslaw mix
- Juice from 2 limes
- ¼ cup red onion, chopped
- ¼ cup cilantro, chopped
- 2 tablespoons olive oil

Directions:
1. Put coleslaw mix in a salad bowl.
   Add avocado mash and onions and toss to coat.
2. In a bowl, mix lime juice with salt, pepper, oil, vinegar and stevia and stir well.
3. Add this to salad, toss to coat, sprinkle cilantro and serve.

Enjoy!

Nutrition: calories 100, fat 10, fiber 2, carbs 5, protein 8

Avocado And Egg Salad

You will make it again for sure!

Preparation time: 10 minutes **Cooking time:** 7 minutes **Servings:** 4

Ingredients:

- 4 cups mixed lettuce leaves, torn
- 4 eggs
- 1 avocado, pitted and sliced
- ¼ cup mayonnaise
- 2 teaspoons mustard
- 2 garlic cloves, minced
- 1 tablespoon chives, chopped
- Salt and black pepper to the taste

Directions:

1. Put water in a pot, add some salt, add eggs, bring to a boil over medium high heat, boil for 7 minutes, drain, cool, peel and chop them.
2. In a salad bowl, mix lettuce with eggs and avocado.
3. Add chives and garlic, some salt and pepper and toss to coat.
4. In a bowl, mix mustard with mayo, salt and pepper and stir well.
5. Add this to salad, toss well and serve right away.

Enjoy!

Nutrition: calories 234, fat 12, fiber 4, carbs 7, protein 12

Avocado And Cucumber Salad

You will ask for more! It's such a tasty summer salad!

Preparation time: 10 minutes **Cooking time:** 0 minutes **Servings:** 4

Ingredients:
- 1 small red onion, sliced
- 1 cucumber, sliced
- 2 avocados, pitted, peeled and chopped
- 1 pound cherry tomatoes, halved
- 2 tablespoons olive oil
- ¼ cup cilantro, chopped
- 2 tablespoons lemon juice
- Salt and black pepper to the taste

Directions:
1. In a large salad bowl, mix tomatoes with cucumber, onion and avocado and stir.
2. Add oil, salt, pepper and lemon juice and toss to coat well.
3. Serve cold with cilantro on top.

Enjoy!

Nutrition: calories 140, fat 4, fiber 2, carbs 4, protein 5

Delicious Avocado Soup

You will adore this special and delicious keto soup!

Preparation time: 10 minutes **Cooking time:** 10 minutes **Servings:** 4

Ingredients:
- 2 avocados, pitted, peeled and chopped
- 3 cups chicken stock
- 2 scallions, chopped
- Salt and black pepper to the taste
- 2 tablespoons ghee
- 2/3 cup heavy cream

Directions:
1. Heat up a pot with the ghee over medium heat, add scallions, stir and cook for 2 minutes.
2. Add 2 and ½ cups stock, stir and simmer for 3 minutes.
3. In your blender, mix avocados with the rest of the stock, salt, pepper and heavy cream and pulse well.
4. Add this to the pot, stir well, cook for 2 minutes and season with more salt and pepper.
5. Stir well, ladle into soup bowls and serve.

Enjoy!

Nutrition: calories 332, fat 23, fiber 4, carbs 6, protein 6

Delicious Avocado And Bacon Soup

Have you ever heard about such a delicious keto soup? Then it's time you find out more about it!

Preparation time: 10 minutes **Cooking time:** 10 minutes **Servings:** 4

Ingredients:
- 2 avocados, pitted and cut in halves
- 4 cups chicken stock
- 1/3 cup cilantro, chopped
- Juice of ½ lime
- 1 teaspoon garlic powder
- ½ pound bacon, cooked and chopped
- Salt and black pepper to the taste

Directions:
1. Put stock in a pot and bring to a boil over medium high heat.
2. In your blender, mix avocados with garlic powder, cilantro, lime juice, salt and pepper and blend well.
3. Add this to stock and blend using an immersion blender.
4. Add bacon, more salt and pepper the taste, stir, cook for 3 minutes, ladle into soup bowls and serve.

Enjoy!

Nutrition: calories 300, fat 23, fiber 5, carbs 6, protein 17

Thai Avocado Soup

This is a great and exotic soup!

Preparation time: 10 minutes **Cooking time:** 10 minutes **Servings:** 4

Ingredients:
- 1 cup coconut milk
- 2 teaspoons Thai green curry paste
- 1 avocado, pitted, peeled and chopped
- 1 tablespoon cilantro, chopped
- Salt and black pepper to the taste
- 2 cups veggie stock
- Lime wedges for serving

Directions:
1. In your blender, mix avocado with salt, pepper, curry paste and coconut milk and pulse well.
2. Transfer this to a pot and heat up over medium heat.
3. Add stock, stir, bring to a simmer and cook for 5 minutes.
4. Add cilantro, more salt and pepper, stir, cook for 1 minute more, ladle into soup bowls and serve with lime wedges on the side.

Enjoy!

Nutrition: calories 240, fat 4, fiber 2, carbs 6, protein 12

Simple Arugula Salad

It's light and very tasty! Try it for dinner!

Preparation time: 10 minutes **Cooking time:** 0 minutes **Servings:** 4

Ingredients:
- 1 white onion, chopped
- 1 tablespoon vinegar
- 1 cup hot water
- 1 bunch baby arugula
- ¼ cup walnuts, chopped
- 2 tablespoons cilantro, chopped
- 2 garlic cloves, minced
- 2 tablespoons olive oil
- Salt and black pepper to the taste
- 1 tablespoon lemon juice

Directions:
1. In a bowl, mix water with vinegar, add onion, leave aside for 5 minutes, drain well and press.
2. In a salad bowl, mix arugula with walnuts and onion and stir.
3. Add garlic, salt, pepper, lemon juice, cilantro and oil, toss well and serve.

Enjoy!

Nutrition: calories 200, fat 2, fiber 1, carbs 5, protein 7

Arugula Soup

You have to try this great keto soup as soon as you can!

Preparation time: 10 minutes **Cooking time:** 13 minutes **Servings:** 6

Ingredients:
- 1 yellow onion, chopped
- 1 tablespoon olive oil
- 2 garlic cloves, minced
- ½ cup coconut milk
- 10 ounces baby arugula
- ¼ cup mixed mint, tarragon and parsley
- 2 tablespoons chives, chopped
- 4 tablespoons coconut milk yogurt
- 6 cups chicken stock
- Salt and black pepper to the taste

Directions:
1. Heat up a pot with the oil over medium high heat, add onion and garlic, stir and cook for 5 minutes.
2. Add stock and milk, stir and bring to a simmer.
3. Add arugula, tarragon, parsley and mint, stir and cook everything for 6 minutes.
4. Add coconut yogurt, salt, pepper and chives, stir, cook for 2 minutes, divide into soup bowls and serve.

Enjoy!

Nutrition: calories 200, fat 4, fiber 2, carbs 6, protein 10

Arugula And Broccoli Soup

It's one of our favorite soups!

Preparation time: 10 minutes **Cooking time:** 20 minutes **Servings:** 4

Ingredients:
- 1 small yellow onion, chopped
- 1 tablespoon olive oil
- 1 garlic clove, minced
- 1 broccoli head, florets separated
- Salt and black pepper to the taste
- 2 and ½ cups veggie stock
- 1 teaspoon cumin, ground
- Juice of ½ lemon
- 1 cup arugula leaves

Directions:

1. Heat up a pot with the oil over medium high heat, add onions, stir and cook for 4 minutes.
2. Add garlic, stir and cook for 1 minute.
3. Add broccoli, cumin, salt and pepper, stir and cook for 4 minutes.
4. Add stock, stir and cook for 8 minutes.
5. Blend soup using an immersion blender, add half of the arugula and blend again.
6. Add the rest of the arugula, stir and heat up the soup again.
7. Add lemon juice, stir, ladle into soup bowls and serve.

Enjoy!

Nutrition: calories 150, fat 3, fiber 1, carbs 3, protein 7

Delicious Zucchini Cream

This is a keto comfort food you will enjoy for sure!

Preparation time: 10 minutes **Cooking time:** 25 minutes **Servings:** 8

Ingredients:

- 6 zucchinis, cut in halves and then sliced
- Salt and black pepper to the taste
- 1 tablespoon ghee
- 28 ounces veggie stock
- 1 teaspoon oregano, dried
- ½ cup yellow onion, chopped
- 3 garlic cloves, minced
- 2 ounces parmesan, grated
- ¾ cup heavy cream

Directions:

1. Heat up a pot with the ghee over medium high heat, add onion, stir and cook for 4 minutes.
2. Add garlic, stir and cook for 2 minutes more.
3. Add zucchinis, stir and cook for 3 minutes.
4. Add stock, stir, bring to a boil and simmer over medium heat for 15 minutes.
5. Add oregano, salt and pepper, stir, take off heat and blend using an immersion blender.
6. Heat up soup again, add heavy cream, stir and bring to a simmer.
7. Add parmesan, stir, take off heat, ladle into bowls and serve right away.

Enjoy!

Nutrition: calories 160, fat 4, fiber 2, carbs 4, protein 8

Zucchini And Avocado Soup

This keto soup is full of tasty ingredient and healthy elements!

Preparation time: 10 minutes **Cooking time:** 15 minutes **Servings:** 4

Ingredients:
- 1 big avocado, pitted, peeled and chopped
- 4 scallions, chopped
- 1 teaspoon ginger, grated
- 2 tablespoons avocado oil
- Salt and black pepper to the taste
- 2 zucchinis, chopped
- 29 ounces veggie stock
- 1 garlic clove, minced
- 1 cup water
- 1 tablespoon lemon juice
- 1 red bell pepper, chopped

Directions:
1. Heat up a pot with the oil over medium heat, add onions, stir and cook for 3 minutes.
2. Add garlic and ginger, stir and cook for 1 minute.
3. Add zucchini, salt, pepper, water and stock, stir, bring to a boil, cover pot and cook for 10 minutes.
4. Take off heat, leave soup aside for a couple of minutes, add avocado, stir, blend everything using an immersion blender and heat up again.
5. Add more salt and pepper, bell pepper and lemon juice, stir, heat up soup again, ladle into soup bowls and serve.

Enjoy!

Nutrition: calories 154, fat 12, fiber 3, carbs 5, protein 4

Swiss Chard Pie

You will always remember this amazing taste!

Preparation time: 10 minutes **Cooking time:** 45 minutes **Servings:** 12

Ingredients:

- 8 cups Swiss chard, chopped
- ½ cup onion, chopped
- 1 tablespoon olive oil
- 1 garlic clove, minced
- Salt and black pepper to the taste
- 3 eggs
- 2 cups ricotta cheese
- 1 cup mozzarella, shredded
- A pinch of nutmeg
- ¼ cup parmesan, grated
- 1 pound sausage, chopped

Directions:

1. Heat up a pan with the oil over medium heat, add onions and garlic, stir and cook for 3 minutes.
2. Add Swiss chard, stir and cook for 5 minutes more.
3. Add salt, pepper and nutmeg, stir, take off heat and leave aside for a few minutes.
4. In a bowl, whisk eggs with mozzarella, parmesan and ricotta and stir well.
5. Add Swiss chard mix and stir well.
6. Spread sausage meat on the bottom of a pie pan and press well.
7. Add Swiss chard and eggs mix, spread well, introduce in the oven at 350 degrees F and bake for 35 minutes.
8. Leave pie aside to cool down, slice and serve it.

Enjoy!

Nutrition: calories 332, fat 23, fiber 3, carbs 4, protein 23

Swiss Chard Salad

This keto salad is perfect for a quick dinner!

Preparation time: 10 minutes **Cooking time:** 20 minutes **Servings:** 4

Ingredients:
- 1 bunch Swiss chard, cut into strips
- 2 tablespoons avocado oil
- 1 small yellow onion, chopped
- A pinch of red pepper flakes
- ¼ cup pine nuts, toasted
- ¼ cup raisins
- 1 tablespoon balsamic vinegar
- Salt and black pepper to the taste

Directions:
1. Heat up a pan with the oil over medium heat, add chard and onions, stir and cook for 5 minutes.
2. Add salt, pepper and pepper flakes, stir and cook for 3 minutes more.
3. Put raisins in a bowl, add water to cover them, heat them up in your microwave for 1 minute, leave aside for 5 minutes and drain them well.
4. Add raisins and pine nuts to the pan, also add vinegar, stir, cook for 3 minutes more, divide between plates and serve.

Enjoy!

Nutrition: calories 120, fat 2, fiber 1, carbs 4, protein 8

Green Salad

You must try this keto salad!

Preparation time: 10 minutes **Cooking time:** 0 minutes **Servings:** 4

Ingredients:

- 4 handfuls grapes, halved
- 1 bunch Swiss chard, chopped
- 1 avocado, pitted, peeled and cubed
- Salt and black pepper to the taste
- 2 tablespoons avocado oil
- 1 tablespoon mustard
- 7 sage leaves, chopped
- 1 garlic clove, minced

Directions:

1. In a salad bowl, mix Swiss chard with grapes and avocado cubes.
2. In a bowl, mix mustard with oil, sage, garlic, salt and pepper and whisk well.
3. Add this to salad, toss to coat well and serve.

Enjoy!

Nutrition: calories 120, fat 2, fiber 1, carbs 4, protein 5

Catalan Style Greens

This veggie keto dish is just great!

Preparation time: 10 minutes **Cooking time:** 15 minutes **Servings:** 4

Ingredients:

- 1 apple, cored and chopped
- 1 yellow onion, sliced
- 3 tablespoons avocado oil
- ¼ cup raisins
- 6 garlic cloves, chopped
- ¼ cup pine nuts, toasted
- ¼ cup balsamic vinegar
- 5 cups mixed spinach and chard
- Salt and black pepper to the taste
- A pinch of nutmeg

Directions:

1. Heat up a pan with the oil over medium high heat, add onion, stir and cook for 3 minutes.
2. Add apple, stir and cook for 4 minutes more.
3. Add garlic, stir and cook for 1 minute.
4. Add raisins, vinegar and mixed spinach and chard, stir and cook for 5 minutes.
5. Add nutmeg, salt and pepper, stir, cook for a few seconds more, divide between plates and serve.

Enjoy!

Nutrition: calories 120, fat 1, fiber 2, carbs 3, protein 6

Swiss Chard Soup

This is very hearty and rich!

Preparation time: 10 minutes **Cooking time:** 35 minutes **Servings:** 12

Ingredients:

- 4 cups Swiss chard, chopped
- 4 cups chicken breast, cooked and shredded
- 2 cups water
- 1 cup mushrooms, sliced
- 1 tablespoon garlic, minced
- 1 tablespoon coconut oil, melted
- ¼ cup onion, chopped
- 8 cups chicken stock
- 2 cups yellow squash, chopped
- 1 cup green beans, cut into medium pieces
- 2 tablespoons vinegar
- ¼ cup basil, chopped
- Salt and black pepper to the taste
- 4 bacon slices, chopped
- ¼ cup sundried tomatoes, chopped

Directions:

1. Heat up a pot with the oil over medium high heat, add bacon, stir and cook for 2 minutes.
   Add tomatoes, garlic, onions and mushrooms, stir and cook for 5 minutes.
2. Add water, stock and chicken, stir and cook for 15 minutes.
3. Add Swiss chard, green beans, squash, salt and pepper, stir and cook for 10 minutes more.
4. Add vinegar, basil, more salt and pepper if needed, stir, ladle into soup bowls and serve.

Enjoy!

Nutrition: calories 140, fat 4, fiber 2, carbs 4, protein 18

Special Swiss Chard Soup

It is so amazing!

Preparation time: 10 minutes **Cooking time:** 2 hours and 10 minutes **Servings:** 4

Ingredients:
- 1 red onion, chopped
- 1 bunch Swiss chard, chopped
- 1 yellow squash, chopped
- 1 zucchini, chopped
- 1 green bell pepper, chopped
- Salt and black pepper to the taste
- 6 carrots, chopped
- 4 cups tomatoes, chopped
- 1 cup cauliflower florets, chopped
- 1 cup green beans, chopped
- 6 cups chicken stock
- 7 ounces canned tomato paste
- 2 cups water
- 1 pound sausage, chopped
- 2 garlic cloves, minced
- 2 teaspoons thyme, chopped
- 1 teaspoon rosemary, dried
- 1 tablespoon fennel, minced
- ½ teaspoon red pepper flakes
- Some grated parmesan for serving

Directions:
1. Heat up a pan over medium high heat, add sausage and garlic, stir and cook until it browns and transfer along with its juices to your slow cooker.
2. Add onion, Swiss chard, squash, bell pepper, zucchini, carrots, tomatoes, cauliflower, green beans, tomato paste, stock, water, thyme, fennel, rosemary, pepper flakes, salt and pepper, stir, cover and cook on High for 2 hours.
3. Uncover pot, stir soup, ladle into bowls, sprinkle parmesan on

top and serve.

Enjoy!

Nutrition: calories 150, fat 8, fiber 2, carbs 4, protein 9

Roasted Tomato Cream

It will make your day a lot easier!

Preparation time: 10 minutes **Cooking time:** 1 hour **Servings:** 8

Ingredients:
- 1 jalapeno pepper, chopped
- 4 garlic cloves, minced
- 2 pounds cherry tomatoes, cut in halves
- 1 yellow onion, cut into wedges
- Salt and black pepper to the taste
- ¼ cup olive oil
- ½ teaspoon oregano, dried
- 4 cups chicken stock
- ¼ cup basil, chopped
- ½ cup parmesan, grated

Directions:
1. Spread tomatoes and onion in a baking dish.
   Add garlic and chili pepper, season with salt, pepper and oregano and drizzle the oil.
2. Toss to coat and bake in the oven at 425 degrees F for 30 minutes.
3. Take tomatoes mix out of the oven, transfer to a pot, add stock and heat everything up over medium high heat.
4. Bring to a boil, cover pot, reduce heat and simmer for 20 minutes.
5. Blend using an immersion blender, add salt and pepper to the taste and basil, stir and ladle into soup bowls.
6. Sprinkle parmesan on top and serve.

Enjoy!

Nutrition: calories 140, fat 2, fiber 2, carbs 5, protein 8

Eggplant Soup

This is just what you needed today!

Preparation time: 10 minutes **Cooking time:** 50 minutes **Servings:** 4

Ingredients:

- 4 tomatoes
- 1 teaspoon garlic, minced
- ¼ yellow onion, chopped
- Salt and black pepper to the taste
- 2 cups chicken stock
- 1 bay leaf
- ½ cup heavy cream
- 2 tablespoons basil, chopped
- 4 tablespoons parmesan, grated
- 1 tablespoon olive oil
- 1 eggplant, chopped

Directions:

1. Spread eggplant pieces on a baking sheet, mix with oil, onion, garlic, salt and pepper, introduce in the oven at 400 degrees F and bake for 15 minutes.
2. Put water in a pot, bring to a boil over medium heat, add tomatoes, steam them for 1 minutes, peel them and chop.
3. Take eggplant mix out of the oven and transfer to a pot.
4. Add tomatoes, stock, bay leaf, salt and pepper, stir, bring to a boil and simmer for 30 minutes.
5. Add heavy cream, basil and parmesan, stir, ladle into soup bowls and serve.

Enjoy!

Nutrition: calories 180, fat 2, fiber 3, carbs 5, protein 10

Eggplant Stew

This is perfect for a family meal!

Preparation time: 10 minutes **Cooking time:** 30 minutes **Servings:** 4

Ingredients:
- 1 red onion, chopped
- 2 garlic cloves, chopped
- 1 bunch parsley, chopped
- Salt and black pepper to the taste
- 1 teaspoon oregano, dried
- 2 eggplants, cut into medium chunks
- 2 tablespoons olive oil
- 2 tablespoons capers, chopped
- 1 handful green olives, pitted and sliced
- 5 tomatoes, chopped
- 3 tablespoons herb vinegar

Directions:
1. Heat up a pot with the oil over medium heat, add eggplant, oregano, salt and pepper, stir and cook for 5 minutes.
2. Add garlic, onion and parsley, stir and cook for 4 minutes.
3. Add capers, olives, vinegar and tomatoes, stir and cook for 15 minutes.
4. Add more salt and pepper if needed, stir, divide into bowls and serve.

Enjoy!

Nutrition: calories 200, fat 13, fiber 3, carbs 5, protein 7

Roasted Bell Peppers Soup

This is not just very delicious! It's keto and healthy as well!

Preparation time: 10 minutes **Cooking time:** 15 minutes **Servings:** 6

Ingredients:

- 12 ounces roasted bell peppers, chopped
- 2 tablespoons olive oil
- 2 garlic cloves, minced
- 29 ounces canned chicken stock
- Salt and black pepper to the taste
- 7 ounces water
- 2/3 cup heavy cream
- 1 yellow onion, chopped
- ¼ cup parmesan, grated
- 2 celery stalks, chopped

Directions:

1. Heat up a pot with the oil over medium heat, add onion, garlic, celery, some salt and pepper, stir and cook for 8 minutes.
2. Add bell peppers, water and stock, stir, bring to a boil, cover, reduce heat and simmer for 5 minutes.
3. Use an immersion blender to puree the soup, then add more salt, pepper and cream, stir, bring to a boil and take off heat.
4. Ladle into bowls, sprinkle parmesan and serve.

Enjoy!

Nutrition: calories 176, fat 13, fiber 1, carbs 4, protein 6

Delicious Cabbage Soup

This delicious cabbage soup will become your new favorite keto soup really soon!

Preparation time: 10 minutes **Cooking time:** 45 minutes **Servings:** 8

Ingredients:
- 1 garlic clove, minced
- 1 cabbage head, chopped
- 2 pounds beef, ground
- 1 yellow onion, chopped
- 1 teaspoon cumin
- 4 bouillon cubes
- Salt and black pepper to the taste
- 10 ounces canned tomatoes and green chilies
- 4 cups water

Directions:
1. Heat up a pan over medium heat, add beef, stir and brown for a few minutes.
2. Add onion, stir, cook for 4 minutes more and transfer to a pot.
3. Heat up, add cabbage, cumin, garlic, bouillon cubes, tomatoes and chilies and water, stir, bring to a boil over high heat, cover, reduce temperature and cook for 40 minutes.
4. Season with salt and pepper, stir, ladle into soup bowls and serve.

Enjoy!

Nutrition: calories 200, fat 3, fiber 2, carbs 6, protein 8

Amazing Asparagus And Browned Butter

This keto dish is very delicious and it also looks wonderful!

Preparation time: 10 minutes **Cooking time:** 15 minutes **Servings:** 4

Ingredients:

- 5 ounces butter
- 1 tablespoon avocado oil
- 1 and ½ pounds asparagus, trimmed
- 1 and ½ tablespoons lemon juice
- A pinch of cayenne pepper
- 8 tablespoons sour cream
- Salt and black pepper to the taste
- 3 ounces parmesan, grated
- 4 eggs

Directions:

1. Heat up a pan with 2 ounces butter over medium high heat, add eggs, some salt and pepper, stir and scramble them.
2. Transfer eggs to a blender, add parmesan, sour cream, salt, pepper and cayenne pepper and blend everything well.
3. Heat up a pan with the oil over medium high heat, add asparagus, salt and pepper, roast for a few minutes, transfer to a plate and leave them aside.
4. Heat up the pan again with the rest of the butter over medium high heat, stir until it's brown, take off heat, add lemon juice and stir well.
5. Heat up the butter again, return asparagus, toss to coat, heat up well and divide between plates.
6. Add blended eggs on top and serve.

Enjoy!

Nutrition: calories 160, fat 7, fiber 2, carbs 6, protein 10

Simple Asparagus Fries

These will be ready in only 10 minutes!

Preparation time: 10 minutes **Cooking time:** 10 minutes **Servings:** 2

Ingredients:
- ¼ cup parmesan, grated
- 16 asparagus spears, trimmed
- 1 egg, whisked
- ½ teaspoon onion powder
- 2 ounces pork rinds

Directions:
1. Crush pork rinds and put them in a bowl.
2. Add onion powder and cheese and stir everything.
3. Roll asparagus spears in egg, then dip them in pork rind mix and arrange them all on a lined baking sheet.
4. Introduce in the oven at 425 degrees F and bake for 10 minutes.
5. Divide between plates and serve them with some sour cream on the side.

Enjoy!

Nutrition: calories 120, fat 2, fiber 2, carbs 5, protein 8

Crispy Radishes

It's a great keto idea!

Preparation time: 10 minutes **Cooking time:** 20 minutes **Servings:** 4

Ingredients:
- Cooking spray
- 15 radishes, sliced
- Salt and black pepper to the taste
- 1 tablespoon chives, chopped

Directions:
1. Arrange radish slices on a lined baking sheet and spray them with cooking oil.
2. Season with salt and pepper and sprinkle chives, introduce in the oven at 375 degrees F and bake for 10 minutes.
3. Flip them and bake for 10 minutes more.
4. Serve them cold.

Enjoy!

Nutrition: calories 30, fat 1, fiber 0.4, carbs 1, protein 0.1

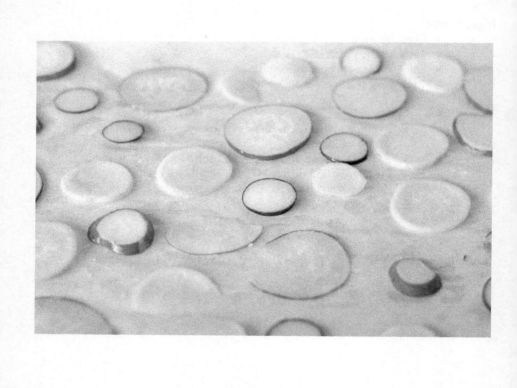

Creamy Radishes

It's a creamy and tasty keto veggie dish!

Preparation time: 10 minutes **Cooking time:** 25 minutes **Servings:** 1

Ingredients:
- 7 ounces radishes, cut in halves
- 2 tablespoons sour cream
- 2 bacon slices
- 1 tablespoon green onion, chopped
- 1 tablespoon cheddar cheese, grated
- Hot sauce to the taste
- Salt and black pepper to the taste

Directions:
1. Put radishes into a pot, add water to cover, bring to a boil over medium heat, cook them for 10 minutes and drain.
2. Heat up a pan over medium high heat, add bacon, cook until it's crispy, transfer to paper towels, drain grease, crumble and leave aside.
3. Return pan to medium heat, add radishes, stir and sauté them for 7 minutes.
4. Add onion, salt, pepper, hot sauce and sour cream, stir and cook for 7 minutes more.
5. Transfer to a plate, top with crumbled bacon and cheddar cheese and serve.

Enjoy!

Nutrition: calories 340, fat 23, fiber 3, carbs 6, protein 15

Radish Soup

Oh my God! This tastes divine!

Preparation time: 10 minutes **Cooking time:** 20 minutes **Servings:** 4

Ingredients:
- 2 bunches radishes, cut in quarters
- Salt and black pepper to the taste
- 6 cups chicken stock
- 2 stalks celery, chopped
- 3 tablespoons coconut oil
- 6 garlic cloves, minced
- 1 yellow onion, chopped

Directions:

1. Heat up a pot with the oil over medium heat, add onion, celery and garlic, stir and cook for 5 minutes.
2. Add radishes, stock, salt and pepper, stir, bring to a boil, cover and simmer for 15 minutes.
3. Divide into soup bowls and serve.

Enjoy!

Nutrition: calories 120, fat 2, fiber 1, carbs 3, protein 10

Radish Hash Browns

Do you want to learn how to make this tasty keto dish? Then, pay attention.

Preparation time: 10 minutes **Cooking time:** 10 minutes **Servings:** 4

Ingredients:
- ½ teaspoon onion powder
- 1 pound radishes, shredded
- ½ teaspoon garlic powder
- Salt and black pepper to the taste
- 4 eggs
- 1/3 cup parmesan, grated

Directions:

1. In a bowl, mix radishes with salt, pepper, onion and garlic powder, eggs and parmesan and stir well.
2. Spread this on a lined baking sheet, introduce in the oven at 375 degrees F and bake for 10 minutes.

Enjoy!
3. Divide hash browns between plates and serve.

Nutrition: calories 80, fat 5, fiber 2, carbs 5, protein 7

Conclusion

This is really a life changing cookbook. It shows you everything you need to know about the Ketogenic diet and it helps you get started.

You now know some of the best and most popular Ketogenic recipes in the world.

We have something for everyone's taste!

So, don't hesitate too much and start your new life as a follower of the Ketogenic diet!

Get your hands on this special recipes collection and start cooking in this new, exciting and healthy way!

Have a lot of fun and enjoy your Ketogenic diet!